D0340815

THE JAPANESE
ART OF LOVE

First HarperCollins Edition

Library of Congress number available on request

ISBN 0-06-251081-9

94 95 96 97 98 XXX 10 9 8 7 6 5 4 3 2 1

WARNING: With the prevalence of AIDS and other sexually transmitted diseases, if you do not practice safe sex you are risking your life and your partner's life.

THE JAPANESE ART OF LOVE

HarperSanFrancisco

A Division of HarperCollins*Publishers*

INTRODUCTION

'The union of male and female, of man and woman, symbolizes the union of the gods themselves at the moment when the world was created.' These words - stressing the symbolic even sacramental significance of sex; rendering impossible any sense of shame or guilt - come from the very first 'pillow book' to bear that name. From a Western perspective it is a difficult idea, yet it permeates Eastern thought and religion and it is the key to understanding the erotic art of Japan.

The first pillow book was written during the Kamakura period (1192-1333) as an aid in the sexual education of young women. There had been earlier erotic manuals, usually based upon Chinese originals, but The Pillow Book with its evocative title and clever format was entirely Japanese.

Eroticism is to Japanese culture what vulcanology is to Japanese geography: a fiery constant underlying everything. The erotic lava flow has had its ebbs and flows: ebbing with the first advent of Buddhism, with censorship under the Shoguns, with Westernization; flowing during the Heian dynasty, in the wealthy monasteries; and finally erupting in 'The Floating World' of Edo, which became modern Tokyo. Even in periods of suppression the erotic core remained, symbolized by the massive phalluses carved from a single tree trunk which occupy the centre of ancient Shinto shrines.

In this book we look at different aspects of Japanese eroticism, both sacred and profane. There are fragments of ancient creation myths and poems by the fifteenth-century Zen Buddhist monk Ikkyu; also included are traditional sexual aphorisms and the poignant songs which geishas wrote to delight their clients. The illustrations are monochrome woodblocks from the numerous sex manuals which have been produced in Japan over the centuries, and shunga - the coloured woodblocks of 'The Floating World.'

Shunga prints are the fiercest erotic art any culture has ever produced: 'the animal frenzies of the flesh!' wrote a startled Edmond de Goncourt, 'the fury of copulation as if transported by rage.' The artists who produced shunga lived in the pleasure districts of the great cities. Here, in the seventeenth and eighteenth centuries, a highly cultured and wealthy bourgeoisie devoted itself entirely to pleasure, especially sex. Their 'Floating World' took its name from a religious concept: everything is transitory. To understand shunga, with its giant genitalia and copious secretions, we need to look further than an artistic exaggeration designed to heighten the erotic charge. This is part of it, of course, but there is another, deeper, level of meaning. Sex is our spark of the divine: through sex we recreate ourselves as the gods once created us and we know something of the pleasure they knew then. Sex is vitally important - quite literally - and we equate importance with largeness. Penises in shunga are analagous to episcopal mitres: when we stand in for gods we must appear larger than ourselves.

In the beginning Izanagi (the first male) and Izanami (the first female) stood on the rainbow bridge of heaven and watched the lightning lance thrust down into the waters of chaos. The foam around the jewelled lance solidified to become the first island of Japan. Soon Izanagi and Izanami learned how to imitate the act of creation with their own bodies, and from them came the whole world.

CREATION MYTH

The dance of the goddess Ame-no-Uzume grew wilder as she recalled a thousand orgasms she had enjoyed: her nipples stiffened and she felt her sex open when she remembered the phalluses of the countless lovers who had penetrated her. When at last she brought herself to the crisis, she opened her clothes to reveal herself to the kami: wet to the knees, her sex throbbing with joy.

THE LEGEND OF AME-NO-UZUME

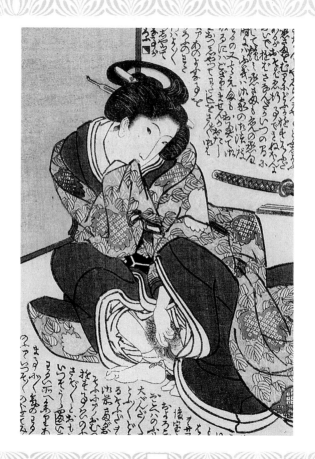

Dream-wandering in the garden of beautiful Mori,
A plum blossom in the bed, faith at the heart
                                                    of the flower.
My mouth is filled with the pure fragrance of that
                                            shallow stream:
Dusk and the shades of the moon as we make
                                            our new song.

                                                    IKKYU

'*Mistress, someone has drawn a mushroom on our front door!*'
'*Here, take this paper and go and rub it out.*'

'Mistress, I rubbed it very hard but it just got bigger!'
'Then that is no mushroom, is it dear?'

SEVENTEENTH-CENTURY JOKE

戯絵
地獄

有時江海有時山
世外道人名利間
夜々鴛鴦禅榻被
風流私語一身閑

Sometimes rivers and oceans, sometimes mountains.
I am an unworldly hermit, apart from fame
and profit.
Night after night, like mandarin ducks, under the
covers on a Zen bed:
That feeling, talking intimately, totally relaxed.

IKKYU

The device of the two copper plums
With silver in them
Slowly and very slowly
Satisfies. Just as all finishes
Dew falls on my clenched hand.
I would rather the bean flowered yellow
And he were here!

GEISHA SONG

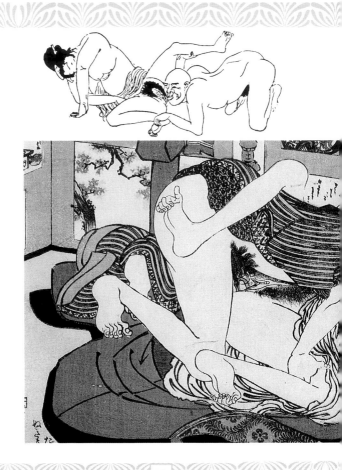

A woman may choose to remove all her pubic hair or she may leave an attractive crown at the front. Depilation is better if she likes to anoint her sex with honey and flower water to make licking more delicious.

PILLOW BOOK

KAWAI, KAWAI
(My dear, my dear)
The firefly singing not
Burns in silence;
She suffers more
Than the loud insect who says:
'Kawai, kawai!'
Why have I given all my soul
To a man without sincerity?
I regret it. I rather regret it.

GEISHA SONG

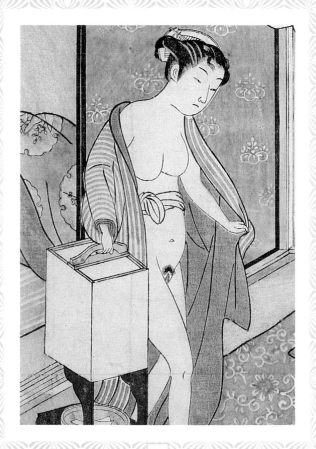

臨済児孫不識禅
正伝真个瞎驢辺
雲雨三生六十劫
秋風一夜百千年

Rinzai's disciples don't understand Zen,
The truth was passed down to this blind donkey,

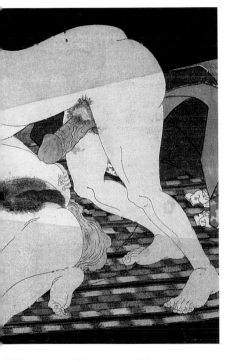

Making love for three lifetimes, ten eons;
One night's autumn breeze, a thousand centuries.

IKKYU

Deep in the boudoir, how much poetry.
A song before the wind-blown flowers, the purity of
this fragrant banquet.
Making love on the bed, a feeling of the
river and the sea.
To spend the rest of our lives like mandarin ducks,
at ease on the water.

IKKYU

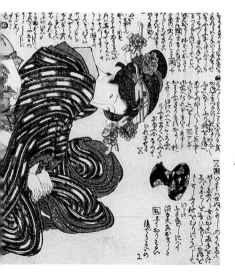

洞房深處幾詩情
歌吹花前芳宴清
雪雨枕頭江海意
鴛鴦水宿逆殘生

MYOSOTIS

If I clasp my hands, my sleeve:
Dew and perfume and colour.
His picture remains in absence
Myosotis, memory.
If he flowered on a branch
I would plant him,
And love him every
Lonely hour.

GEISHA SONG

Gaze at Chu's pavilion and then climb up to it.
At midnight on the precious bed, between dreams of
sad longing

Her flower opens beneath the plum tree's branch
A graceful nymph between her thighs.

IKKYU

JOY

Visitor this evening
We run up the long corridor
Clicking of clogs.

Only one man,
Only one person to be loved.

I go back to my room,
Retreat, honour,
Lacquered pillow,
Silence.

I hear the watchman's rattle,
Laughter in the next room.

GEISHA SONG

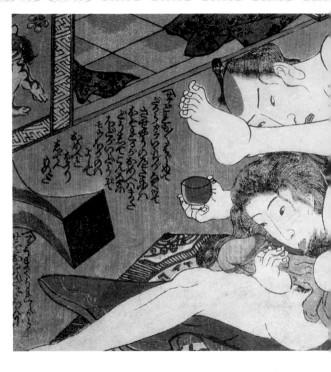

Few penises sleep so soundly they cannot be awakened with a kiss - but this kiss is not the peck of a bird, it is

the tongue, palate and lips of a hungry calf noisily
sucking at a teat.

PILLOW BOOK

My hand, would that it resembled Mori's hand
My faithful lady's, the mistress of love's caress.
When I am ill she heals my precious stalk
And brings joy to my circle of followers.

IKKYU

且喜我金茎象
発病治玉茎萠
自信公風流主
我手何似森手

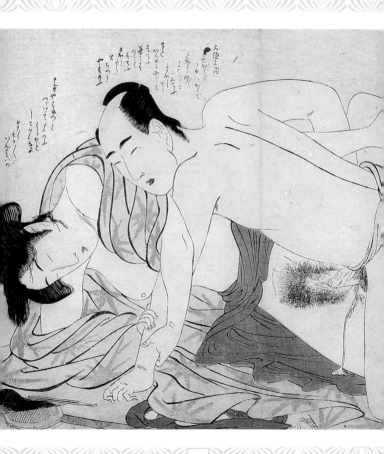

HIS PRETTY GESTURE

Because of his pretty gesture
I have fallen completely in love with him.

My letter written in common character
Will be worth more than a verbal message.
But I may not hold him yet.
I am going to drink sake all night
Without bothering to warm it.

I lie down on the floor
Just where I am, and sleep.
I wake with a start
To hear the night watch crying:
'Fire, take care of fire'.

GEISHA SONG

Whispers, bashfulness and a pledge.
We sing of love and make promises for
                    three lives to come.

絶勝溷山戴角情

生身堕在畜生道

風流吟罷約三生

密啓自慙私語盟

We may fall to the way of beasts while still alive,
But I shall surpass in passion the horned abbot of Kuei.

IKKYU

FAITH

I am the ordinary cherry tree
Whose flower is single.
It blossoms in the plain.

I am not one of those double cherry trees!

GEISHA SONG

A woman has two mouths and several vaginas: a husband may be brought to ecstasy between her buttocks or her breasts, or between her thighs or in her armpit. Always pay attention to cleanliness and use lubricating creams.

PILLOW BOOK

TWO FAN GAME

Two thrown fans
Have fallen across each other
It is a good sign.

I see two mortals close in each other's arms
Like two leaves fallen together.

Will he be a fine chrysanthemum?
I will put him in a vase
And look at him
He will be plum blossom
Having both scent and colour.

GEISHA SONG

The guests have left, the music ended, there is no sound;
One cannot tell when she will awake from this
profound sleep;

誰聞日午打三更
覩面当機胡蝶戲
不知極睡幾時驚
客散曲終無一声

Now as I watch, a butterfly plays.
Listen, the bell strikes midnight at noon.

IKKYU

BEFORE MY BIRDS

I moan for love
Before my birds.
They also are in a cage.

My small complaints
Are sorry like mouse cries.
The birds hop forward to tease me
And I like it
Being so shut in.

The sake is cold
Because my torment
Makes me inefficient.
There is such a thing as great grief,
Such a thing as
Being shut in.

GEISHA SONG

盲森夜々伴吟身
被底鴛鴦私語新
新約慈尊三会暁
本居古仏万般春

Blind Mori night after night sings with me
Under the covers, like mandarin ducks, new
                              intimate talk
Making promises to be together till the dawning of
                    Maitreya's salvation.
At the home of this old buddha all is spring.

                                        IKKYU

けのおもいのふかきをねてもさめてもわすれしや

Talk in the reed hut reaches the Shou-yang Palace.
Butterflies elegantly sport, their excitement
never spent.

茆蘆話到壽陽宮
胡蝶優遊興不空
枕上梅花窓外月
吟魂夜々約春風

On the bed, a plum blossom, outside my window,
the moon.
Singing souls, night after night, entwined in the
spring breeze.

IKKYU

PREDICTION

A hole in the paper wall
Who has been so guilty?
Through it I hear the breaking of a samisen string,

Meaning had luck.
Yet the prediction-seller says
That mine is excellent.

GEISHA SONG

Dreams

Under the unnecessarily large
Mosquito curtain

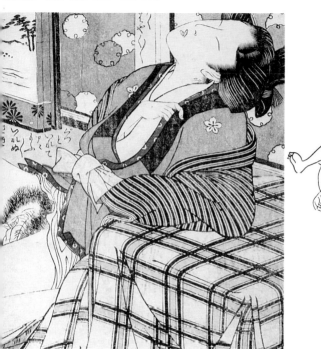

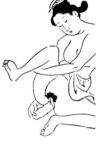

My little heart
Is fiercer than a nightlight.

GEISHA SONG

水仙華

香与梅花修約盟
風流瑤草両三茎
凌波仙子茶雲雨
碧海青天夜々情

JONQUIL

Her perfume mixes with my plum blossom; we

pledge ourselves.

A caress like two or three stalks of Yao grass,

She makes love like a graceful river nymph.

This feeling night after night: the sapphire sea,

the azure sky.

IKKYU

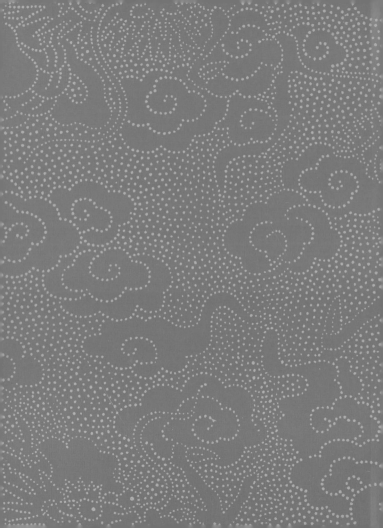